SPORTS

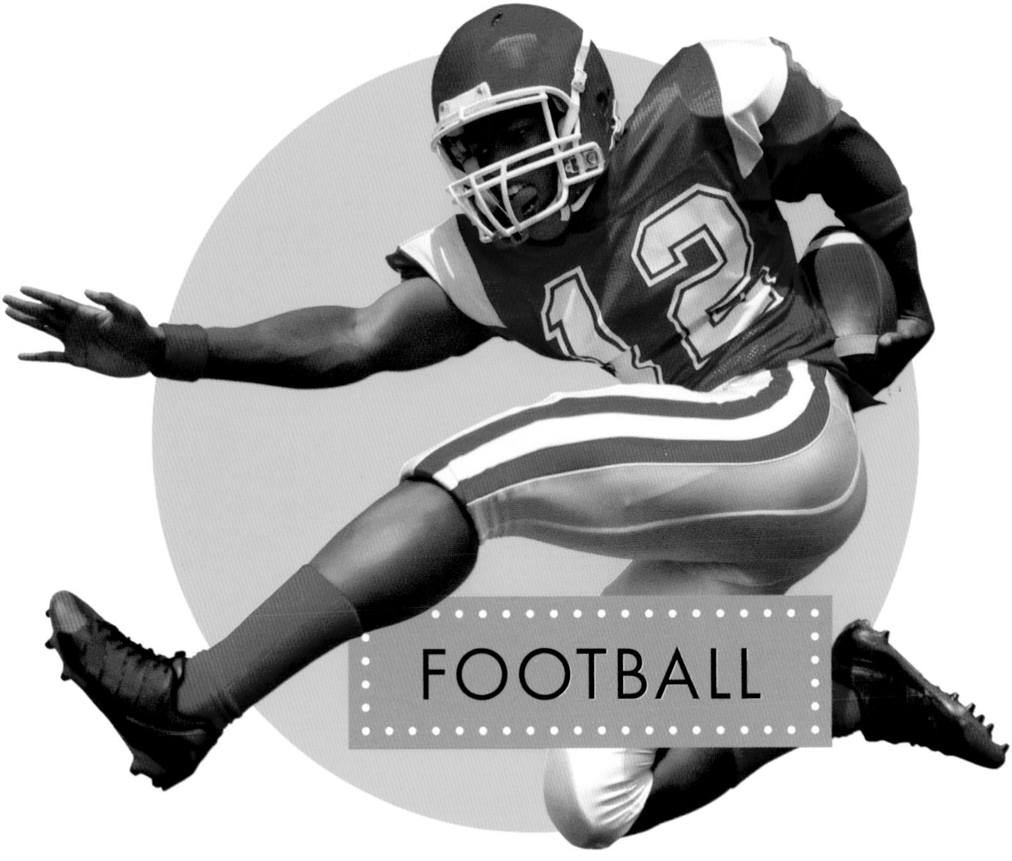

FOOTBALL

by Mari Schuh

AMICUS | AMICUS INK

helmet

goalposts

Look for these
words and pictures
as you read.

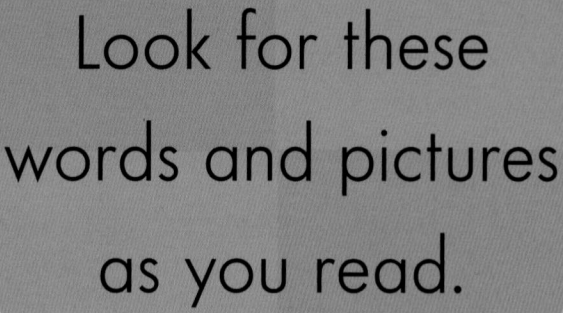

flag

quarterback

A player kicks the ball.
A football game starts.
Let's watch!

Two teams play.
Each team has 11 players
on the field.

helmet

Do you see the helmet?

It has the team logo on it.

Go, team!

Do you see the goalposts?
A player kicks the ball
between the posts.
It's a field goal!

goalposts

flag

Do you see the flag?
The game stops.
A player broke a rule.

Do you see the quarterback?
He throws the ball far.
Way to go!

quarterback

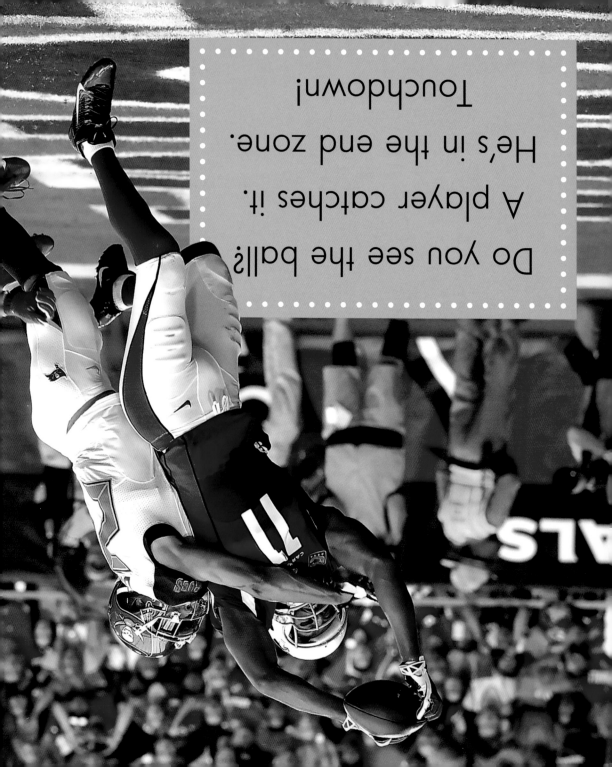

Do you see the ball?
A player catches it.
He's in the end zone.
Touchdown!

helmet

Do you see the helmet?
It has the team logo on it.
Go, team!

goalposts

Do you see the goalposts?
A player kicks the ball
between the posts.
It's a field goal!

helmet

goal posts

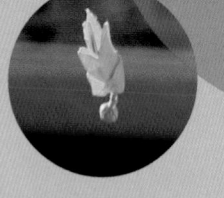

Did you find?

flag

quarterback

Do you see the flag?
The game stops.
A player broke a rule.

flag

Do you see the quarterback?
He throws the ball far.
Way to go!

quarterback

Spot is published by Amicus and Amicus Ink
P.O. Box 1329, Mankato, MN 56002
www.amicuspublishing.us

Library of Congress Cataloging-in-Publication Data
Names: Schuh, Mari C., 1975- author.
Title: Football / by Mari Schuh.
Description: Mankato, Minnesota : Amicus, 2018. | Series: Spot.
  Sports | Audience: K to Grade 3.
Identifiers: LCCN 2016057196 (print) | LCCN 2016058334
  (ebook) | ISBN 9781681510866 (library binding) | ISBN
  9781681522050 (pbk.) | ISBN 9781681511764 (ebook)
Subjects: LCSH: Football--United States--Juvenile literature. |
Picture puzzles--Juvenile literature.
Classification: LCC GV950.7 .S38 2018 (print) | LCC GV950.7
(ebook) | DDC 796.332--dc23
LC record available at https://lccn.loc.gov/2016057196

Printed in China

HC 10 9 8 7 6 5 4 3 2 1
PB 10 9 8 7 6 5 4 3 2 1

To Dad — M.S.

Rebecca Glaser, editor
Deb Miner, series designer
Aubrey Harper, book designer
Holly Young, photo researcher

Photos by: AP Photo/Greg Trott,
8–9, Lynne Sladky, 10–11, David
Stluka, 12–13; Getty Images/Doug
Benc, 4–5, Rob Carr, 6–7, Norm
Hall, 14–15; iStock/Yobro10,
cover, 16, GeorgePeters, 1;
Shutterstock/Aspen Photo, 3

FOOTBALL